I Dreamed

the Ocean

Froze

I Dreamed the Ocean Froze

Poems by Victoria McCallum

2023

Printed in the United States of America.

Published by Parrotfish Press, Bellingham, Washington.
  Visit the author's website at www.parrotfishpress.com

ISBN 979-8-2181-8379-0
Library of Congress Control Number: 2023905916

Cover photo: Markus Trienke, *Pack Ice in Kulusuk Bay, Greenland, 2017.* Creative Commons, used with attribution.

Design: Catherine Wallace, Wordworthy Media Services.
  Visit the designer's website at www.wordworthymedia.com

For Lantz

Praise for *I Dreamed the Ocean Froze:*

"From a kangaroo's watch to genuflections, Victoria McCallum has opened a door to let her audience peek into her world—even if it didn't always really exist. I appreciate how her poems read like a menagerie of memories: family, history, and natural images drawn with words on the page."

—**J.L. Wright**, author of *Unadoptable Joy: A Memoir in Poetry and Prose* and *Homeless Joy: An Expose in Poetry*

•••

"Sip a cup of holy water, spiced with a cube of surrealism, and settle in with *I Dreamed the Ocean Froze.* McCallum's unique poetic style will take you places you've never imagined—from ancient Rome to Planet Z—with snippets of giggling nuns and goddesses and the underwater mother. You'll want to carry this book around, often saying to a friend, 'Listen to this!' You'll want to give a copy to your best friend."

—**C.J. Prince,** poet, author of *Mother, May I?* and co-author of *Catching My Breath* and the upcoming *Pandamndemic*

•••

"Victoria's poems are swaggeringly, purposefully unmoored from any tidy narrative of how things are. She lives in this collection of Tygers, continents, sea anemones, rubies, checkers, stilettos, and licorice as a rebuttal to any disbelief in the rough magic of becoming—a sensuous full-grown Cassandra in the child's shoes her mother bought. Her poems kick those shoes off the page and she runs on ink-stained feet as her shouts and whispers echo in a time zone all hers. To follow her is to find our own tilted and turning kaleidoscope of the senses."

—**Tere Harrison**, writer and spoken word performer in one-woman shows often with more than one woman in them

"The true mystery of the world is the visible, not the invisible."

—Oscar Wilde

Victoria's Metaphorical Surrealism

After experiencing one of Victoria's poems, people will often ask "what is that poem about?" People anticipating realism with maybe a dash of mysticism may be left puzzled.

Andre Breton explained surrealism as a verbal expression of the actual process of thought in which the unconscious is constantly trying to break through into consciousness. As surrealism developed in writing and then painting, it often led to juxtaposed images that are outside the realm of rational analysis. Think of Dali's painting *The Persistence of Memory* with its limp clocks draped over bare tree branches. The effects on the rational mind are of surprise and uneasiness. Victoria achieves these same effects of consciousness with her images in poems like "The Sea Anemone" or "My Mother is a Medusa Monster."

Victoria's artistic method includes adding a metaphorical component to her surrealism. However, her metaphors are often incomplete and unstated. For example, "Snow in Los Angeles" creates a surrealistic image of snow in Southern California, while it implies the unstated multiple metaphorical meanings of snow—of purity and cleansing, of freezing and dying, but also of a blanket or an insulation, of revealing and concealing. In "Blue Speckled Bowl" the bowl itself becomes a container for memories and even the infinite possibilities of the whole wide world.

For a garnishing effect Victoria often uses whimsy in her comic poems such as "The Goddess of Candy" and "Big-Footed Woman." Indeed, the reader should be prepared as her ever unfolding imagination may take you anywhere. So read on and enjoy the journey through Victoria's world of metaphorical surrealism.

Table of Contents

I Live in a Boxcar

I live in a boxcar
pulled from the rails
hid in the pine
on the mountain
by the lake.

I live in a boxcar
with a round window
drilled and pounded out
during one hundred nights
of wind and rain.

I sit on their cot and eat potato soup.

You live in a treehouse in town.
You light your candle at night
and read The Book of Wisdom.
You are a carpenter.
You build houses in your dreams,
drink Coors,
and make love to Vietnamese women.

I live in a boxcar.
Tomorrow I'll carpet my floor
with pine needles and rose petals.
In August I'll make curtains,
lavender ones.
I'll pick blackberries
and crush them
on a flat, white stone
and stain the gauze
that will blow out of my round window.

We shower in the morning and they check us for lice.

He lives in the park
of wild, thornless roses and dripping fountains.
He holds the silver lid, his shield,
and with the tree branch, his sword,
he jabs at the paper
searching for his deed from the King
who says the park is his fiefdom,
the ducks are his peasants,
the pond is full of snapping turtles,
and all poachers will be guillotined.

Yesterday they gave me new shoes. They're too big,
but I pretend elephants follow me everywhere.

I live in a boxcar
up on the lilac mountain by the firefly lake.
You should see it.
Yes, come Wednesday
for red clover tea.
I'll boil the water
and say the words.
You won't get sick.
Sorry, but I don't have any cake.
You must bring one.

She lives on the corner
across from Farmer's Insurance.
She wears a soiled white nightgown
and a blue blanket.
People toss coins

in her empty tin of Shirley Jean Christmas candy
that sits on a bundle of clothes
in her Safeway shopping cart
that holds, she thinks, the baby Jesus.
You live in a treehouse.
He lives in the park.
She lives on the corner.
But I—
I live in a boxcar.
I have a home.
I have a home.

The Boast

Tell me again
ping pong poetry
in rhyme and rhythm
what I knew
but didn't know
that I did,
so
hypnotize me
then with your quick wrist flick
and your Eucharist moon glow
as you, poetry, overpower prose.

Let's Make Tea You Said

(Hollywood Riviera, 1956)

Let's make tea you said to Mother
when you were seven and your little brother,
and I, your baby sister, were tucked away at last.
Too big for afternoon naps, you my eldest brother,
you, the little man, struck the match,
your magic wand, and swoosh—the blue flames leaped,
then circled round the iron holes.
What will it be, Mother?
Orange pekoe, Earl Grey, Darjeeling?

Not content with Fiesta, you choose
chintzware—Royal Winton, made in England.
Silver spoons, festooned with roses,
lie gleaming against the counter's
sky blue tile while you pour
milk in a tiny glass creamer.
Then you carry a plate of Lorna Doones
to the table by the windows that face the Pacific.

Now sipping your tea, you stare at the plate
of posies—blue bells, tiny violets, swollen roses—
and think of all the stories you and Mother have read.
Your apartment on Paseo de la Concha hasn't a secret
    garden.
Outside grow bougainvillea, cactus, and scrappy roses.
But beyond, oh beyond the field across the street,
lie the sand and the ocean and China too far away to see!
You think of Ping hunting for little fishes on the Yangtze
    River.
You, too, would brave a spank not to miss this ocean, this
    tea!
Today the distant waves look like white sheets

tucking you in gently, gently while the gulls cry.

Apricot light filters through the palm trees and warms
    your mother's lips, the teacups' lips, your plate, your
    hands.
You bite into another Lorna Doone and smile at Mother.
Last week she baked gingerbread bears and orange
    pinwheels.
Next week for your birthday she's promised cherry
    blossoms,
cookies that look like sugared stars pierced with red
    hearts.

Father at work,
brother and sister asleep.
You appraise all of these sweets,
Mother, Lorna Doones, orange pekoe,
the palm trees, the sun, the gulls, the ocean—
one long burnished afternoon at tea.

My Father's Kangaroo

He calls to me—
the kangaroo porcelain figurine
that sits atop my dad's dresser.
After school, I hear the kangaroo's voice
urging me to visit.
I study his Little Lulu eyes,
his foxlike face, his mustache smile
while he whispers, "no teacher troubles
here, lass, no taunting classmates."
In school I like painting pictures
best so I admire the kangaroo's colors—
burnt sienna and cream and smoky gray—
and how black singes both the tip of his tail
and his upright triangular ears,
and also I admire how his black boxing
glove paws guard his open pouch tray where my dad
deposits his pennies and buffalo nickels.
When I pick up a worn gold cufflink
embossed with an ugly old man's face,
the kangaroo says, "That originally
was a coin your father found
while time traveling in ancient Rome."
I point to a pair of sunglasses in a red
case tucked in a slit in the kangaroo's side.
"Why your father wore those glasses to decode
Nazi messages when he was stationed in Paris."
I finger a gold and silver bracelet watch
that's hung on the kangaroo's tail.
"Oh, yes, that watch is a trifle heavy,"
the kangaroo admits, "but I can bear the weight
until your father's next mission to Planet Z.

You see, my dear, the watch's ticking
translates the Z creatures' speech."
"Are you from Planet Z?" I ask the kangaroo.
"No, I'm from Planet Y. There is a *big* difference!"

The Sea Anemone

A sea anemone lives
inside my mother's mouth.
Its purple tentacles wave
as she speaks.
They look like arms that
say, "Yes, you must mind me!"
I will do anything my mother
asks, but sometimes I forget
and spill orange juice
or invite my friends over
when she hasn't cleaned.
Then the sea anemone squirts
me until my eyes sting.
I say five more Hail Marys
at bedtime while my mother
listens, but when she leaves
I cannot fall asleep.

My father never hears my prayers.
He doesn't believe in the Trinity.
Every year, when he kneels beside me
at Christmas Mass, he repeats after the priest,
"Jesus Christ, the son of our Lord,"
as if he's swearing.
No one hears him.
Last month he went back to Toronto.
Even though my father sends me postcards
and signs them with hugs and kisses,
I'm afraid to ask him
if he ever saw the sea anemone.
Last week I told my two brothers
about the sea anemone, but

they laughed and said,
"We saw you chewing on those
violets in the garden last night."

Today my brothers and I explore
the tide pools near Malaga Cove.
Shocking pink sea anemones grow
on the rocks and I'm careful not
to step on them because I'm barefoot.
I wonder if these sea anemones
belong to other mouths. Maybe
the sea anemones have the day off
while the mothers go to their dentists.
What if only my mother has a sea anemone
and what if no one else ever sees it?
My mother's face is reflected in the tidal
pool and her seaweed hair pops as I step on it.

The face of Venus appears in the water.
She grows larger.
She looks like the goddess in the painting
who is standing naked on a huge shell,
her golden hair waving in the wind.
My oldest brother likes to look
at her in my father's art book.
The reflected Venus is holding a baby
like Mary holds Jesus, but
the baby's wrapped in a swirling
pink cloth so it can't be Jesus.
I like Venus better than Mary.
I will pray to her tonight.
I know Venus will know
the sea anemone is in my mother's mouth.

Mockingbird Love

Just when I think the mating season's over,
the mockingbirds resume their shrill staccato calls
like the monk who tells me not to dance
alone in my lion suit in the cathedral.
He says join the other nuns, but I don't like
their dance—too many virgin gloves
tentatively touching fingertips and smothering giggles

and what about their ritual of swirling
black skirts and bowing heads and kissing that crucifix?
I want to douse them with red wine and blooden
their white wings only I'm hypnotized
by the stained-glass windows above spinning cobalt
blue, yellow ochre, violet, peach and crimson.

Now the kaleidoscope eyes of God fragment us into confetti
while Tolstoy throws condoms and rice at the nymphs
plucking the big swan on the mosaic sunburst floor.
I leave for my laundry, but am stung by omnipresent
mosquitoes at the Mass Camp for Unlearning Literacy
where giraffes chew satin ribbons, spit out

statues of saints, and quilt packages of music scores:
first Bach, then *Oklahoma!* and
"Rolling, rolling, rolling rawhide!"
the mockingbirds sing; the chimpanzees keep time
by shaking gourds filled with midget dinosaurs.
I ask, "How many eggs will hatch and build Viking ships?"

No mockingbird will answer, but Wayne Newton
croons "Red Roses for a Blue Lady"

so I think I want to be in the cartoon—
all 3 by 3 inches—when George Washington's false teeth
cha·cha·cha over burnt ground in Guatemala
and I'm left wondering, what is the sound of black lace?

The Goddess of Candy

Goddess of love and goddess of wisdom:
you sashay your colors,
    (Aphrodite—alizarin red and gold
     Athena—cerulean blue and silver)
and you whisper promises
    (Aphrodite says, *Die in satin sheets!*
     Athena says, *Live in gilded manuscripts!*).
Sisters, tantalize no more.
You cannot outdo the goddess of candy.
She's the fairest one.

Think she anemic and toothless?
Her honey hair rivals Demeter's,
and her eyes, her sapphire eyes
look deeper than the Mediterranean.
Come sample her blessings.
Her cornucopia overflows
with caramels, butterscotch, and licorice.
The goddess herself?
Why bittersweet chocolates drop from her lips,
peppermints kiss her nipples,
taffy unfurls from her fingertips,
and gummy fishes swim between her toes.

Behold her lollipop bouquets!
Choose cherry or grape or sour apple;
don't forget mango-orange or vanilla-lime.
Aphrodite, why ask Mars for his bar?
She'll give you the Milky Way,
for the goddess of candy
satisfies any yen for yin.

Athena, beware of substitutes:
nix on poppies and lotus blossoms,
Helen-as-prize or Greece-in-ruins.
Submit to sweetness, you two;
surrender to candy divine.

Poet's Cobweb

"Your name was in the teachers' bulletin," Phil tells me. "The front office wants your file back. Some teacher has it, and they're not sure which one." I'm puzzled. I want to see the bulletin only Phil can't find the copy. He likes to go through Miss Howard's wastebasket in homeroom. "I think it was the day before yesterday," he finally insists. "When you were absent. I'm sure your name was in it."

I think over the last few days. I think of how my grandmother made tapioca pudding every day for months, so that now, decades later, my father refuses to eat it. I think of how my grandmother liked to recite William Blake at odd moments such as

Tyger! Tyger! burning bright
In the forests of the night

when she passed the potatoes. I think of how my father keeps saying I'm like her and giving me that eye roll. Then I think of the poem I just wrote for the yearbook contest and how my poem wasn't cheerful, so maybe the signatures won't like that. I wrote of roots that grow in jars and look like purple veins getting high on sugar solution.

A few weeks pass. I find excuses to look through Miss Howard's wastebasket but never find any teacher bulletins. My poem isn't selected. Jellyfish's is. I get to hear it. Miss Howard reads the poem aloud to our class while Jellyfish glows. "Now that was so inspirational," Miss Howard coos after she reads the last line. Yep, that's it, I think. Jellyfish's poem doesn't insist on gloom. After all, we're only seventh graders. We won't live exclusively on canned ham and beets—at least, not this year. Last September, I didn't see custom-made bomb shelters at the Pomona Fair like I did when I was six and wore pink plastic headbands. I study Jellyfish while her friends congratulate her just like they did last week when she scored another home run. And Jellyfish doesn't have any zits! Plus she wears cashmere and corduroy *ensembles* while I wear ice cube bracelets and dropped-waist shifts patterned with turtles and sea horses and neon green polka dots. My mother buys me those dresses at Newberry's and my classmates guess their origins and sneer.

Today in art class, Kenny puts rubber cement in my hair and after school it takes me two or three hours to comb it out. The next day, my journalism class rejects my idea for a column called "Poet's Cobweb." I'd even drawn the spider and a few sample spinsters, but the kids laugh at it. Maybe I should have drawn a big bug with the spider eating it and then I'd probably have gotten at least some votes from the boys.

Two weeks later, I give Mr. Patterson, my journalism teacher, a woodcut Christmas card that I made in Girl Scouts. The card's simple—just a picture of a royal blue angel bordered with stars and printed on thick white linen paper—but Mr. Patterson looks at my card like I just puked all over his desk. Meanwhile Jellyfish and the others string tinsel and fake holly around the room for our Christmas party. That's it, I realize. I didn't write tinsel for the yearbook contest. Teachers like Mr. Patterson and Miss Howard expect tinsel and I didn't deliver because—I wrote about heroin for the contest!

When I go home, my brother Gordon, a ninth grader, invites me into his room to play checkers. He likes to play checkers with me since he almost never wins when he plays chess with our brother Gavin, an eleventh grader and track star. While we play, I study Gordon's Phantom of the Opera model that he's glued together but hasn't painted yet. Phantom's face is more interesting than his mask, I decide as my brother beats me again and again. After he's won seven games in a row, he begs me to play just one more game. By now I can see the checkerboard clearly just by closing my eyes. "Nope," I say, "I'm ending this marathon." Then I go into my room, sit down at my desk, and begin writing another poem, discovering—my own *fearful symmetry.*

I Become Go-Go

(California, 1966)

Saturday afternoon at Zody's discount house I become go-go,
the go-go girl guided to the rack,
who selects a black floral, vinyl hip-hugger mini
steps into skirt and cinches its wide matching belt
then lunges, kicks, twirls
in fluorescent lime-lighted dressing room cage.

Imagine
the go-go girl hops on motor scooter
(her skirt's tiny poppies, primroses
and violets glow neon on Mod midnight).
Outside London, her scooter collides
into Rolls carrying Russian agents and traitor Brits.
Go-go girl scampers over hedges
slips inside stone ancestral manse
seizes glass vial (filled with formula for world's demise)
turns and kick dances spies away.

I hand a ten to Zody's cashier
with sprayed beehive and Cleopatra eyes.

Monday morning I become go-go
tuck gold poor boy T-shirt
inside vinyl, hip hugger mini
slither into yellow fishnet hose
don red suede Mary Janes
and black meter-maid cap.
Before biology class Rick yells,
"Go-go stole a tablecloth from Poppa Pete's
last night and now she's wearing it!"
Mr. Finn smiles and asks why I cut my slicker in half.

After school smoker boys lounging in field spit on vinyl
    mini as I pass by.

Monday evening, a Windex bottle and scissors meet go-go.
I make book covers for
ALM French Level One
and *Beginning Algebra*.
I save the remaining vinyl
for *The Complete Novels of Jane Austen*.
Then at bedtime, I open *Pride and Prejudice*
and Elizabeth Bennet becomes go-go.

The Stuffed Bird

In her crimson coat
my mother looks like a stuffed bird
wired to a branch in a wild game museum.
She sits beside me in church
and answers the priest
and looks at me because
I do not answer him.
I can no longer follow the Mass.
I do not remember the prayers.
I do not understand the guitars
or the English words.
Before, when I was ten,
the Latin words
smelled like incense,
but burned like cigarettes
quickly, in my stomach.

My mother kneels at the altar,
her tongue posed for the wafer.
I kneel alone at the pew and remember
how the stuffed bird's colors—emerald green, mustard,
turquoise, and violet—looked iridescent
on her wing, but how she was
crimson, just crimson from a distance.

I saw the stuffed bird
in a wild game museum when I was ten.
A young boy was running away from his father
and saw her, too, and stopped to touch her.
The stuffed bird didn't move,
but she blessed the boy with her tanzanite eyes

and pierced him with a silver thread
that only he and I could see.
Then the father caught his son
and slapped him hard,
but the boy didn't cry
since he was charmed by the bird.

I do not know the names of birds.
Last month I described the stuffed bird
to my friend, the ornithologist,
but I didn't tell him she's my mother.
He said such a bird does not exist,
but he was wrong,
so I drew him a picture
and painted it to get the colors right.
He said again, no such bird,
but he kept the painting and
had me sign it.

My mother crosses herself with
holy water and steps outside where
another woman admires her crimson coat.
She needs a peacock hat
to set it off, I say.
My mother looks at my feet and asks
why I never wear the shoes she buys me.
They cost her enough; don't I remember?
My shoes line the pathway from
the church entrance to the parking lot.
As the priest greets his parishioners
he picks up several pairs
and hands them to me.

I drop the shoes in the holy water.
My mother blushes then,
but the priest smiles and blesses me.

I run to my mother's car and
open it with my key
and drive off
while my mother talks to the priest.
I drive for my real mother,
the stuffed bird.
I drive to her tanzanite eyes
and her silver thread
and her iridescent wing.

Georgia

Georgia wears
bright blue hummingbirds
and persimmon-colored flowers
like a painting, not a blouse,
a Gauguin gone awry
over her man-sized belly
and narrow hips.

But she's not a Tahitian queen;
she's the king in Paradise Manor.
Beatrice, the eighty-nine-year-old virgin,
won't wheel herself into the dining room
when she sees Georgia. Leroy, the gardener
with Parkinson's disease, takes his sandwich
to his room when Georgia looks at him.

Georgia stands by the dining room window.
She rocks back on her heels,
forward on her toes,
and chants,
    Gimme my Weyerhaeuser money.
    I want my Weyerhaeuser money.
    Gimme my Weyerhaeuser money.
    Now!

I make coffee in the kitchen.
Georgia peers inside and fingers
her short silver hair,
slicked back like
a twenties tycoon.

She says,
> *Gimme a cup of coffee.*
> *Gimme a cup of coffee*
> *and some choc-late cake.*
> *I want some choc-late cake.*
> *Gimme a cup of coffee*
> *and some choc-late cake.*

Georgia looks at me with her glacier eyes.
She's six inches taller,
seventy pounds heavier,
and there's only a silver tiered cart between us
as high as my chest.
I hand her the coffee
which is really a mango
laced with lotus fruit
because
there's never any chocolate cake for Georgia.

Georgia drinks her coffee fast—
six or seven gulps—lots of fake cream.
But I really see her peel away the mango
and devour it and the lotus fruit.
I really see the juice from the fruit
staining her hummingbirds
and her persimmon-colored flowers.
When she bangs her plastic cup
on the cart, returns to the window,
and holds her belly
and laughs and laughs and laughs,
I know it's beatitude.

Cora the cook twitters,
 They say Georgia was a lesbian.
Betty the nurse chuckles,
 Could be
before she samples Cora's apple crisp.
But Betty has another name for Georgia
when she stirs pink powder in Georgia's juice.

In the hallway when Georgia hovers
over the water fountain
and whispers the incantation
 My water, my water, my water!
crocodiles slither away and sun
themselves on banks of jungle flowers
while Georgia floats on her back
and drinks papaya and passion juice.

Salmon Have Too Much Press

(PDX, 1988)

I shouldn't be on this plane. I should be back in the freezer
case in the Safeway in West Salem, not bound for L.A.
Snug as possibly snug one can be while lying frozen next
to red snapper, salmon, swordfish, scallops, and squid.
Communicating telepathically through cellophane. I'm
colorful—blue and yellow and green, streaked with apricot
and splashed with rose. A parrotfish they say with an
orange and green-lidded eye. Isabel, the woman who bought
me, didn't have an ice chest, so she stuffed me inside
her black canvas bag next to her spiral notebooks, *The
Oregonian*, and three gothic novels. The widely spaced teeth
from her plastic hairbrush pierce my scales. Her cartridge
pen leaks on me like an octopus in a rage.

I hear people discussing my smell. They think I stink. A
woman about fifty dressed in crisp, white cotton declares,
"Quite horrible, really. And considering the fares they
charge." I don't think they have anything to complain
about. Look at the real culprit. See that bleached blonde
in the silver-sequined mini dress with the silver stockings
and the five-inch glitter heels? Why she's painting her
nails purple and silver with black dots. Who is she? A
manicurist, perhaps, operating on herself, perfecting
techniques. Her nail polish is giving me a headache—yes,
right above my eyes before the rise of my dorsal fin.

Isabel seems oblivious to the passengers' complaints and
the blonde's nail polish. She's reading one of her gothics
and has come to the part where the heroine is bathing
her feet in the hero's fishpond when the villain, the hero's
cousin, appears and hungers for more than the sight of

her trim white ankles. He says, "If you like my cousin's fishpond, you should see his lake. Come, I'll take you there." Isabel rather likes the villain, so when the Delta steward asks her what she wants to drink, Isabel replies, without looking up from her gothic, "Whatever you're having."

Why didn't Isabel drop me off at the soup kitchen before she boarded the shuttle bus bound for the Portland airport? Or why didn't she leave me in the freezer? Or why didn't they barbecue me in Salem? Have a luau in my honor. Roast a pig. Cup up pineapple slices and turn them into edible earrings. Hire seven dancing girls in grass skirts. They could crown me at this luau. Write poems in my honor. Sing songs of the great parrotfish. Salmon have too much press.

Maybe you think I'd rather be cavorting in the coral reefs. Erecting my fins for all the nubile females. Calling, "Hey, pretty baby, lay some eggs my way." And feasting. What feasting! Grinding that coral and eating that algae. Nothing better.

I don't like what Delta is serving for a snack. Mini croissants, cantaloupe cubes, three ounces of O.J., and Bloody Marys for the two henna-haired punkettes in black who have fake I.D. but disarming smiles for the steward who looks like he belongs in a Ralph Lauren ad. He likes their black lipstick. "Now what color is that?" he asks. "Eggplant," one volunteers and giggles.

If Isabel had any guts she would have had me stuffed.

Then I could have modeled for fish vases—big in the Northwest. An Oregon potter immortalizes us. Tastefully. Isabel bought one for her host and hostess, Monty and Judith. It was nothing exotic. Just a blue carp number. But if the potter had seen me—

Isabel keeps seeing fish. Everywhere. In Portland she saw fish posters and fish potholders and fish earrings. In Salem she bought fish magnets to hold down fish recipes on Monty and Judith's refrigerator which she stocked with fish. Last night, Judith brought home a rainbow trout. Isabel said it was too perfect to eat, so she inked it and did a series of fish prints. Isabel could ink my body any time. Now she wouldn't get the brilliance of my colors, but my outlines...

Isabel wonders about her constant fish sightings. She thinks she's not superstitious, but she still believes a fish might be her mascot. She frets over the fish necklace she didn't buy in Portland. It would have been her talisman. Isabel should really stuff me and hang me on her living room wall. I could be her guru.

Me, I'm agnostic. I used to believe in a Superior Being, but then I found out a blue whale is just a blue whale is just a blue whale.

My Mother Is a Medusa Monster

I find a fortune
a yellowed scrap of words typed, not printed
inside a pink box of jasmine tea
Ta Chung Brand
inside a box of journals and graduate school papers and
    Crayolas
transported to Oklahoma from Oregon,
a fortune that I haven't seen in five years,
a fortune reading:
"Mothers are the only goddesses the whole world believes in."
So I stop and consider if it's true,
remembering my own mother
once pretty with auburn hair and seashell ears.
But now her soul, her essence
looks smeared with charcoal
like a soul drawn in catechism class,
a soul floating between Purgatory and Hell.

My mother is not a goddess.
My mother is a Medusa monster.
My mother sticks poison combs in my hair,
tightens and tightens the lace that crisscrosses my belly,
hides poison apples in my fruit bowl.
My mother lights a torch and guides me
through a subterranean passage,
through a cavern she promises is littered
with diamonds, rubies, and sapphires.
But I see only stalactites and stalagmites,
teeth in my mother's womb,
so I run away and she shrieks:
"You thought there'd be what? Jewels?"

My mother hangs funhouse mirrors
in my bathroom, in my bedroom, in my hallway;
then hisses, "Victoria, you're too thin, you're too fat;
your hair's too dark, your hair's too light; you need lipstick,
rouge; comb your hair, wear something tight, show your legs;
marry that lawyer; and goddammit, go to Mass!"

My mother hides an octopus in her strawberry
tinted crown, so that when she hugs me and I respond
the octopus squeezes my head and sucks on my eyes
until I cry, "Yes, you are right. Yes, I am selfish.
Yes, my poetry chapbooks will never be *blockbusters*.
Yes, teaching underprepared college students isn't the
     glamorous career *you* wanted for me.
Yes, that tent dress makes me look six months pregnant.
Yes, I turned him down and he's making six figures now.

Yes, I penned that April Fool's letter from your old flame
     Stanislav.
Yes, I sent Cousin Isabel that twelve-inch purple dildo for
     her bridal shower.
Yes, for ten dollars I patted the bulges of all the manikins
     in Macy's wearing men's bikini briefs right in front of
     Mrs. Kowalski.
Yes, I straddled the stone griffin naked except for my silver
     heels in Aunt Sophie's garden and kissed the griffin
     under the full moon for Cousin Derek's *art* photograph.
Yes, I fucked the Seven Dwarfs, the Frog Prince, Jack on his
     Beanstalk, the Beast, the Giant, and the Big, Bad Wolf.
Yes, I spiked Father McCallister's fruit punch at Cousin
     Isabel's wedding and then seduced him in the rectory at
     midnight,

And yes, I did *that*, too, and Uncle Lech won't leave me alone
  with his German shepherd.

My mother opens her kaleidoscope heart.
It blooms scarlet, olive green, sunflower gold,
but then the cranberry contracts; the silver slivers
until a Thai knife wielding master emerges slicing my
    fingers
as if they were zucchini, carving my mouth into a rosebud
    radish,
scalloping my eyes into cucumber pinwheels and bows
unmasking himself as my mother who says,
    "I want to try that new bistro on 4th Street, so
    we'll go there for your birthday."

The High Priestess Speaks

You bring me apricots
and almonds in a Chinese bowl,
lay lilies at my feet,
stand back, then run away.

Come sit with me;
share the offering.
When you were young you
never swallowed wafers whole.
They stuck inside your mouth and
you'd rescue Christ
with your tongue, but he
always broke into pieces
and you never felt resurrected.

Forgive Christ.
Forgive the priests.
Forgive your mother
and the rest.
Bake your own wafers now
but swallow the sun,
not the moon.
Find the ancient city
in your throat
and speak the lost voices
in your poems.

You can sit between
the dark and the light
columns without fear.
You are the architect of serenity.

My moon, a yellow sickle
in your violet sky,
cuts the weeds back at midnight
and without the stars and the lantern
you can still see.

Big-Footed Woman

Woe to the big-footed woman!
Atlas holds up the world,
but she has one foot in the Adriatic
and the other in the Aegean.

Doubt my words?
Call the roster;
begin with Ella of small feet
embalmed in blinding, crystal blue slippers.
Next comes Dorothy shod in ruby pumps
coveted by the Wicked Witch.
Don't forget Snow White;
her fairest feet sporting Mary Janes
are far lovelier than the Queen's
fat soles housed in mink mules.

In her black stilettos, Barbie clicks
across hardwood floors;
whereas, centuries before,
Chinese princesses totter,
then collapse on silk pillows scattered
en route to the emperor's midday banquets.
(A journey of a thousand yards
ends after twenty baby steps.)
Handmaidens freshen the princesses' bloody bindings.

Questions inevitably arise:
Did the Handsome Prince kiss
Sleeping Beauty's feet before her lips?
Did the Seven Dwarfs finger Snow White's
instep once she succumbed to the poison apple?

And did Ken zip up Barbie's boots before lacing
her black leather bustier and handing her the whip?

The big-footed woman can only imagine
erotic scenarios, for signs keep her out:
    Those whose soles are as wide
    as horses' hooves need not apply.
    Duck-footed women go home.
    Only little feet can crush the King's grapes.

No matter.
The big-footed woman climbs the highlands,
steals sheep from the lowlands.
She hoes, hauls, and harvests;
she hoists megaliths and builds monuments,
her feet becoming wider and wider,
until one day she leaps
across streams and then lakes and then seas.
A goddess she becomes,
a goddess of big feet.

Aphrodite Lies Beneath Wisteria Vines

Centuries ago, across the Atlantic,
nine miles outside Paris,
you and your lover were one:
Two statues, he an insouciant Ares,
and you an indolent Aphrodite,
standing as alabaster sentries in a not-so secret garden.
There flowers bloomed obscenely in a tangle
of honeysuckle and lilacs, purple pansies and
pink camellias, gladioli, roses, and violets.
Giant sunflowers poked their heads above the gates,
witnessing the ladies as milkmaids
    and the lords as shepherds and stable boys.
Amid the perfumed coupling,
how were you to know
the difference between bread and cake
when you yourself never ate?
And costumes for the living—
rags of hemp or silken gowns,
not one cloak or fifteen furs?
Why you and your lover posed naked
until summer's morning glories died.
And when winter roses turned to thorny hands,
no raiment was required; you smoldered still.
L'amour, l'amour, l'amour was enough.
Even the birds never spotted your brow.

But one midnight, on horseback
and on foot, the hungry came
bearing torches for the mansion, swords
for the titled, and axes for the statuary.
Sometime during the fire and the plunder,

the killing and the raping,
your Ares, too, was struck, defaced.
Ashamed, paralyzed, he, a war god without a nose,
didn't defend you, when the ax sang,
and, you goddess, lost your head.

The patriot spoiler, though, worshipping
your perfect breasts, your hips, and your thighs,
spared them; he gave your body to all France,
hoping every maiden—short or tall, beautiful or plain—
could stand behind your form and become an Aphrodite.

Now south of San Francisco, two miles east of Los Altos,
in another garden, you listen beneath the wisteria vines,
your right ear a translucent seashell pressed to damp ground.
Your stone head has rolled close to the house, built
from recycled glass panes and reclaimed redwood beams.
Deep blue bottles lining the kitchen window cast
cobalt shadows on your wide, wondering eyes.
No longer distracted by your marbled urgings,
what do you hear?
Rumblings from the San Andreas fault?
Tidal waves and monsoons far off in the Pacific?
I imagine you, Aphrodite, righting yourself,
your head posed on the porch step,
serenely telling us about earth's next disaster.
Or do you attend to our garden talk
of once again pressing the titled to give
dollars for bread and for books and for pens?

Your Seventh Rosary

(West Los Angeles, 1990)

"Who shot President Kennedy?"
Walter Cronkite asks.
Will we find an answer in our own lifetime;
I wonder.
Will the sealed documents reveal much?

My husband drinks iced tea
and watches the *NOVA* tape
for the second time.

On the bedroom wall, the pale woman
in the zigzag crimson cap
strangles herself with a red
satin chord. I wear her.
She's my bolo.

What can keep your neck warm and your dick dry?
Bright and wide mid-sixties ties. Polite codpieces.

I want to hike the Appalachian Trail
or at least visit Ireland.
But really—
I want to say fuck off to five people,
maybe more.
I'm angry.
I want to say, "Take the one-way ticket to
Manchuria and call me in ten years.
Better yet, write.
Then I know I won't hear from you."
Or—
"After you've said your seventh rosary,
do you take your coffee enema?"

This apartment's a black cloisonne box,
and outside, snow leopards patrol Stoner Park.

I could go north to Mount St. Helens,
but how many times have I been
dusted with volcanic ash?

"You mean the single bullet fantasy?"
my husband says to Walter Cronkite.

If I put in enough *W*, *L*, and *R* sounds,
I'll write a real speech impediment poem.
I try to imagine sounds but taste
colors instead. Blue's the best.

Car accidents.
Cubic zirconia.
Astroturf.
Tanning salons.
Cellular poets in L.A.
Wasted umbrellas hung over from rainy
February nights in Oregon.
How many umbrellas haven't I lost
or broken in eight years?

Consider what you're not using, Victoria:
That jar of alfalfa seeds.
Harriet's advice for painting your walls sunny kitchen
    yellow.
Those five yards of fuchsia brocade.
Your Sheaffer cartridge pen with blue-black
ink filling up canary pads, 8½ by 11.
Or playing jacks by the wasps in the windowsill

at your country school outside Sedalia, Missouri in
November 1963 while your impoverished but Republican
classmates lament our President's passing.

The man is wearing a two-headed donkey hat
and this isn't a children's book.

And then there's
Jackie Kennedy's pink mohair suit with the black lapels
with blood
without Jack.

Red Snowflakes

(Santa Monica, October 1992)

It doesn't do any good when the snowflakes
are red and blue—hot and cold—always the same
on the worn flannel bed sheet and I'm still washing dishes
    and my
husband is still reading another book on the assassination
    of JFK.

Voices travel across the pebbled aquarium and
I can't hear them, though I see the snakes.

Yesterday a squirrel clung to a palm tree
and looked at me with his mouth open before
he disappeared in the fronds.

This morning the ivy shadows lengthen
on the lace curtains and the angels are gone.
Yes,
I look at Walt, at Vincent.
Their postcards are tacked on our
cracked and peeling walls:
Vincent's at his easel,
painting those sunflowers that burst bright
yellow blood on his canvas.
And what about Christmas in his café?
Deep red and emerald green interior,
a test for the color blind.
Or those irises—and their leaves—
spear-shaped like Whitman's grass.
Vincent at 37 dead,
but Walt at 37 still lived and lived and lived.
Walt with his gray beard and his

Panama hat—accepting, loving, forgiving,
embracing, feasting, Walt.

Walt is painting
and Vincent is singing about those old shoes
I wore in Oregon when I was eighteen
and should never have thrown away.
Those black leather shoes—round-toed,
ankle-laced, platform heeled—worn down
until I could not walk straight in them any more.
But does it always come to this, Vincent?
To our shoes, balancing in our shoes?
Can Americans only see red and blue
never violet,
never your iris,
in election year 1992?

Speak of
pant zippers, fetuses, single bullets in Dallas.
What say you, Walt?
I want your voice to write a poem to Jack.

Beads

The mail brings catalogs from fine art museums
addressed to the woman who lived here before,
a woman who liked beads.

I see her stand before her maple bureau
studying a jumble of beaded necklaces
lying on silk scarves and then quickly
twirling a pearl strand up her pale arm
as if it were a spiral staircase to her heart.

Now she holds a glass ruby bead to the light
its hexagon shape a prism
throwing red roses on white walls,
roses that unfold oasis dreams,
visions, French gardens.

And fingering more beads,
she sees a landscape, a world
in each mandala, in each talisman
until she's reading tea leaves in beads:
 You want him back.
 You want him gone.

Each bead a pillow to plump lies
to herself in this pink world of beads.
And each bead a distant city that calls her:
 Vancouver, Montreal, Halifax, Paris, Istanbul!

All of these beads and more dangling before her
like the prince's portrait trapped in a locket
on a charmed bracelet hanging from the ceiling

inside the Beast's enchanted castle
where he's calling her, whispering her
to a green world
beyond her yellow world
of Kmart and Cascade and Dial soap
and wouldn't you like a Hungry Man for dinner?

She crushes marjoram, basil, oregano
and stirs them into a vegetable barley soup,
the beads dancing above the gas flames
peppering her brew
swirling amid the steam.

At the kitchen table, she leafs through the catalogs,
coveting and naming the beads:
    painted porcelain, jade, garnet and gold,
    blue lace agate, onyx, mother-of-pearl,
    lapis lazuli, mosaic glass, rose quartz,
    cloisonné, amethyst, emerald, turquoise.

For she wants a curtain of beads
hanging in her kitchen window
another shielding her bed
another enveloping her bath
while she's cooking, sleeping, bathing
in a rainbow of beads:
    her home a cathedral of beads
    shutting out all but the beads.

Shirts

I look at the shirts hanging
in the closet and think back
to the times he'd bought them,
all cotton shirts in pale shades—lavender,
blue-grey, bleached lemon, muted mauve and
charcoal plaid, blue and white stripes, rose
with peach checks—and how I'd seen
them wear out, the collars and cuffs
frayed, the black ink stained into the front
pockets, the holes in the yoke from his
wrestler's shoulders straining the large
that should have been an extra-large, but size
was sometimes a problem when the shirts came
from India and there were only small, medium,
and large, and after all, cotton still shrinks.

I feel like I've shrunk, too.
But other times, I feel too large as if
I could lift the bar bearing all
the shirts and walk twenty miles and
throw the bar off the cliff, scattering
the shirts, a pastel quilt covering the ocean.

But I don't want the shirts
to be an art performance piece.
I want to buy him new shirts.
I want to buy him shirts for the rest
of his life; even if I'm not with him,
I want to send him shirts wrapped
in blue paper like shirts from a local
laundry, shirts covered with postage from

foreign lands—perfect, exotic, comfortable
shirts—custom shirts commissioned
to fit his shoulders for once.

And looking at his shirts, I remember
how Jay Gatsby's man from England
sent him shirts and how Gatsby piled
dozens and dozens and dozens of these
shirts on a table for Daisy Buchanan to admire.
Daisy, in turn, smothered her head in the shirts
and gushed how she'd " '… never seen such—
such beautiful shirts before.' "

And then I reimagine Fitzgerald's scene
so that Daisy is fingering Gatsby's shirts,
throwing them on his bed, rolling among
the satin and silk and flannel ones herself,
coupling with the shirts and laughing and
laughing and laughing until Daisy's coming
and…

But Daisy wouldn't touch Gatsby's shirts
long enough, or as long as I touched his
shirts, my man's shirts,
when I ironed them for interviews
or when I sewed on those embroidered
patches to cover the ink stains he bled
into his shirts as he wrote those
beautiful sentences into our nights
and into our days.

Across the Continent

Across the continent my lover sleeps.
I peer at him through my spyglass
and behold a Gulliver caught
in tangled snow-white sheets,
breathing…
breathing…
breathing.
In daylight is he a sphinx spewing
wit in torrents of blue-black ink?
Or is he a verdant man napping
in the buttercup, befriending honeybees?
But back to night now,
is he a Galileo outdistancing us all,
knowing how our planets and stars truly link?
Yet if he would awaken and
sense me watching him from faraway,
would he roar,
what is there to look at?
He is only a man sleeping, a sleeping man.
I could make inquiries.
Dispatch a detective.
Brave a telegram.
Ask him myself of his travels
in his dreaming land.
I picture him reclining in a sleigh—
his slumber sweetened with orange blossom pillows
and warmed with quilts of deepest down.
I envision him gliding over a frozen pond
that turns into a frozen lake
that turns into a frozen, ever widening sea.
I imagine all that
only to report once more:
Across the continent he sleeps.

With Sweetness and With Ice

On the *Harrowsmith Country Life* cover
farmhouse lights paint pale yellow
coffins on the periwinkle snow.

Winter in New England looks warmer
than spring in North Redondo.
Jacaranda blossoms and agapanthus lie.

Noon birds of paradise turn
to violet axes on snow white walls.

Petit four cottages, glazed
with rosettes and sugared violets,
come ringed with Saturnalian ice.

And evening hosts a lemon moon
more silvery than golden,
more Eucharist than enchantment.

What do we do with sweetness?
What do we do with ice?

Snow in Los Angeles

Last November I dreamed the ocean froze
and we ice-skated to China.
Last night I dreamed a female lion
approached me in my living room
and growled, threatening to spring;
but I sat still on the sofa
and looked into her agate eyes
until she leaped on the headrest
and embraced me from behind.

Last Christmas in New Hampshire
I walked through minus thirty winds
past three-story white houses
gabled with angels and dwarfed by evergreens.
The northern sunlight gilded the apricot panes
until three p.m. when the sky
and the snow both turned lavender.
Later, as I felt slush in Cambridge
turn to slippery brick, I wanted more snow,
but I had to return to Santa Anas.

Today, a February morning,
I visit my father in Oceanside.
He says it snowed in Pasadena in 1949.
People wouldn't work; they snapped
pictures and chased each other instead.
Dogs dug their noses in the snow,
then shook their heads, showering
the ground with snowflakes.

My father was born in Winnipeg
and has seen the snow.
As he talks I imagine hobos
pouring cherry brandy over snow cones

and burning wood by train
    tracks.
They can't die of exposure
because with Hitler and
    Mussolini dead
everyone thinks we all have
    a wonderful life.

Tonight, upstairs in my
    father's loft,
I try to read, but the words
blur like watercolor.
I turn on the television,
but I can't see the news.
I see her, the lion bounding
across a snow-covered
    overpass, throwing violet
    shadows
on the deserted, blue-white
    lanes,
sprinkling red drops—
    rubies, not blood—
paving her jeweled path to
    the sea.

I wait for it to snow in Los Angeles.

Think in Terms of Sunder

Think in terms of sunder.
Leave behind a continent,
a country, a tongue.

Board the immigrant ship,
as she did:
Wiktorya Kowalska, my namesake,
my blood, my mother's mother
who died before I was born,
who died before she could tell
me tales of Warsaw streets,
of an angry Atlantic, of a century's close.

What did she bequeath me?
A ruby ring too big for my fingers,
a copy of a birth certificate
in a language I cannot read,
a mauve-tinted wedding portrait
of Wiktorya a bride at eighteen.

Can I honor her phantom legacy
with satin words on paper
sewn like her French seams?
Must I only embroider questions?
Or, can I quilt a grandmother
from others' reluctant memories?

They say in the garden, in the kitchen, in the parlor
she worked her artistry with flowers, fruit, and cloth.
I want to inhale her lilacs
that bloomed a towering twenty feet.
I want to taste her *pierniki*,
both the cinnamon stars and the aniseed angels.

I want to hear her curse Hitler and Mussolini
before she downed her nightly shot of vodka.

But Babcia, did you put the coal in my
mother's Christmas stocking?
Did you stop speaking to your sister
because she loved your husband?
Did you ever stop grieving for your Julie,
the two-day-old you baptized then buried?
I do not see your face in my face,
but do I, too, wear your sorrow's corsage?

Think in terms of sunder.
Leave behind a continent,
a country, a tongue.

No Doors, No Windows

My brother Wilfred lives
in a house with no doors,
and last I checked,
with no windows, too.
How does he go out at night?
Does he shape shift
into a vampire mole
that tunnels to and fro?
Or was he that coyote
prowling outside my cottage last night
as I carried in my apples and my oats?
Or was he that midnight bat
last week that circled 'round
and 'round my living room?

Bertram, my oldest brother asked,
"Why cry creature visitations
when our brother evades you so?
Pater and Mater both died, so what
if that beastly Wilfred wants to mourn alone!
But no entrance, no exit to his house?"
the newly minted Lord Bertram scoffed.
"Your fantasies, dear sister, do implode!"

Oh, but a month has passed, and
Wilfred has never answered my knock;
he has never answered my note.
I only asked him to play croquet
as we did when we were little
or to have a chat over tea and toast.

Yesterday afternoon I tried once more;
I walked three miles to Wilfred's home.

And he, in turn, had arranged a Magritte sky
to outline his castle bungalow,
a fortress for a Handsome Prince,
I mused, and not for a Beast inside.
Although I thought it was day,
maybe it was night,
for his porch light glowed a peachy glow
while thick ivy, covering his roof,
hung like dragon tails just above his door.
I pressed his doorbell once, twice and thrice,
but heard not a ring, though black paint
found my finger and my eyes then
found his trompe l'oeil front door
and his trompe l'oeil front windows
on his frescoed bungalow.

Then in tiny print, I read
above the first window to my right:

> *Fold along the perforated lines;*
> *then, if you dare, open the window!*

Immediately I pressed the painted lines
of fresco turning into cardboard window
as if it were an Advent calendar to Wilfred's soul.
But next a lemon window opened into
a persimmon window and then into a boysenberry
window and into more layers and layers and layers
of cardboard painted windows; and, ah,
until that day, I had seen nesting dolls,
but never nesting windows.

But at last, as I folded back smaller
and smaller cardboard windows, I reached

a tiny plaster window that became an owl's eye.
"I am in despair!" I cried to the owl's eye.
Instantly it became a black plastered egg or
maybe a trompe l'oeil pirate's eye patch.
I slowly circled around Wilfred's bungalow,
examining his trompe l'oeil back door
and his trompe l'oeil cellar door and each
and every one of his trompe l'oeil windows.
Weary now, I returned to the front porch
where I nodded to the owl's reappearing eye.
"Goodnight, Owl," I said. "Goodnight!"
And I went home to bed.

A fortnight passed. My cousin Susan visited
Lord Bertram and his Lady, then took tea
at my cottage where she revealed
her uninvited sleuthing scoops:
"Bertram," Susan said, "has mounting gaming debts,
a mistress to keep, and at his manor,
parties planned galore."

The next evening I was sent to dine
at the manor with the Lord and Lady.
Over oysters and his finest French wine,
Bertram agreed that I had paid
for my cottage: "No doubt, no doubt," he said.
"But, out, out, that leach Wilfred must go;
out of my bungalow, for it must be sold!"
His lady hissed, "The last time Wilfred was
at the manor I think he stole some silver."

Early the next morning, Susan's maid delivered
a message at my cottage door: "Miss, the Lord sent

the Sheriff to your brother's bungalow. Please, go!"
The maid then handed me the reins of Bertram's best mare.
Moments later, when I arrived at Wilfred's home, the Sheriff
and his four burly rogues stood atop the ivy-covered roof,
and with a hack here and a hack there, they uncovered
three hidden skylights. As the rogues smashed the glass
and descended through the roof, I discovered
Bertram lurking in the blueberry bushes below.
And oh, how I trembled at the pounding and the shaking
and the shrieking as the Sheriff and his four burly rogues
stormed the princely beast's castle bungalow.

Yet costumed as a porcupine and not to be outmatched,
Wilfred burst through that papier-mache cellar door
that had been a fresco trompe l'oeil.
With a wild whoop, he hopped into a pumpkin coach
hidden behind the wisteria vines, and at once
that pumpkin coach turned into a midnight blue roadster
with a black canvas top. As the car sped away, I swore
that blue roadster had no doors and it had no windows,
for they simply smudged away like charcoal.

I urged the mare forward to follow
my disappearing brother and his disappearing
doors and his disappearing windows,
but the Sheriff, on his white stallion following behind,
grabbed my reins and I tumbled off the horse.

"That's my mare!" Bertram shouted as he trotted up on his
    gelding.
The Sheriff held out his hand while I struggled to right
    myself.
"Forget about her bruises," Bertram said to the Sheriff,

meaning me, not the horse, who had ambled off to graze.
"Shall I press charges for her thievery?" Bertram asked.
I said, "No!" Still the Sheriff and Bertram held me back.
Meanwhile, the four burly rogues on their four black stallions
gave chase to the blue roadster into parts unknown.
And alas, alas, I have seen my brother Wilfred no more.

Another fortnight passed. Cousin Susan has heard rumors
that highwaymen slashed the midnight blue roadster's top,
    dented
its doors, broke its windows, and robbed Wilfred of his gold.
"Or was it the four burly rogues?" she added with a sigh.
Susan sipped her tea and bit her biscuit and reported more:
"Then those brutes, whoever they were, conked Wilfred on
his crown until he bled and bled and bled all alone."

But perhaps, I think—though I do not say
to Cousin Susan nor to Lord Bertram and his Lady—
perhaps Wilfred has wandered far and far away
in another wood, a deeper wood,
where he will construct another house
with no doors and with no windows.

The Blue-White Dress

She says goodbye to the dress
the post-recession 1980s dress
the blue-white, made-in-China dress
the V-collar with cutwork-embroidered bib
   and rounded back collar dress
the knee-length, dropped waist with blue-white sash dress
the short sleeved, not-quite-sailor dress
the crisp cotton, not quite vintage flapper dress
the little girl grown-up dress
but the dress that thirty some years later still fits.
And she remembers the times she wore the dress:

The September morning job interview she bested, knowing
homelessness would not be her fate. The April evening she
read her poems with the others at Beyond Baroque. The
June afternoon tea in Pasadena where she sat inhaling
gardenias and sipping Darjeeling and listening to New
Orleans jazz until,

in an instant, 1986 became 1926 and she was watching
F. Scott Fitzgerald drink gin in what he claimed was
a water glass while Louise Brooks and other starlets
sunned themselves by the pool and Fitzgerald lamented
over Zelda's incessant drinking and why couldn't Zelda
be captivating yet still sensible as she, the young woman
before him, in the blue-white dress who knew how to listen.

Or how in August 1987, invited to a San Francisco
wedding, she, without finery, tied a scarlet silk scarf over
the hips of the blue-white dress, hoping not to disrespect
the bride resplendent in a white lace designer gown. But

after the ceremony, she blinked and found herself drinking
champagne in a 1967 London wedding reception where she
was mistaken for a courier by Russian agents crashing the
party. Was it the scarlet silk scarf that tipped them?

Then how in Seattle in 1988 on a misty May night she
wore the dress again but donned a cobalt blue cloche,
walking quickly to make a Marx Brothers movie playing
at an art house when she bumped into a man with a red
moustache and found herself running through 1928 Paris
streets, pursued by that same man. He thought she was the
psychic who stole his fiancée's diamond and ruby necklace.
Was it the cobalt blue cloche that confused him?

Now back in her time, thirty some years later, she holds
the blue-white dress to her cheek, remembering the swish
        and swirl
of every occasion wearing the dress in her time
and out-of-her time, traveling in the blue-white dress.
She says goodbye to the dress
so that someone else in the thrift shop
can say hello and step into this dress, the blue-white dress.

Go in Peace

I would like someone to invent the quietest leaf blower on
     earth,
a blower whose decibels register below a whisper,
a blower that plays white noise or Mozart or Scarlatti
and I would like this leaf blower to perfume the air with
     rose water or lavender or eucalyptus, not gasoline,
and I would like the optional accessory of headphones filled
     with loud
heavy metal music and the sounds of jackhammers and tile
     saws for
those leaf blower users who miss the high decibels of
     previous models
and, of course, I would like no one else to hear these high
     decibel sounds
from the headphones of those using this optional accessory.
I would like to add another optional accessory of the sound
of one hand clapping or the sound of gently raking leaves
     for those
Zen masters who prefer hand tools, for this new leaf blower
would give them more time to meditate even if it is a
     walking
meditation while blowing away leaves with this new leaf
     blower.

I would like the inventor of the quietest leaf blower to
     bestow the first
model in my hands so that I could blow all the leaves and
     all the conifer needles off our
lane, driveway, garage steps, and porch and thereby end
     my obsession with needles
tracking up the stairs to the kitchen and into all the rooms

of our house since,
as you may have guessed, my husband and I do not now
    use a conventional leaf blower.
I would like to promote a peaceful home as I would no
    longer be ranting
about conifer needles completely carpeting our floors
    and my husband would be spared of this ranting and
my frequent bouts of cursing while vacuuming and
    sweeping endless needles.
I would like an additional feature of programmed but
    thoughtful
subliminal messages of peace, love, and understanding to
    issue from this new leaf blower
and that all my neighbors and I would be positively
    affected by these messages.
I would like my neighbors to be so enraptured by my quiet,
    peaceful leaf blower that
they would want to discard their loud leaf blowers and use
    mine or order their own.
I would like them *not* to request the additional accessory of
    headphones
filled with loud heavy metal music and the sounds of
    jackhammers and tile saws;
however, I must be tolerant since these sounds might be
    their pet sounds.

I would like everyone in Sudden Valley, everyone in
    Bellingham, everyone in Whatcom
County, everyone in Washington, everyone in the United
    States, everyone in North
Korea, everyone in the Russian Federation, everyone in the
    world who uses a leaf blower

or who wants to use or to buy a leaf blower to be issued this
        whisper blower—I will
henceforth call it the peace blower—so that I do not feel
        tortured and everyone else does
not feel tortured by the deafening decibels of conventional
        leaf blowers.
I would like everyone who uses this universal peace blower
        to become not only soothed
but empowered by the new leaf blower's additional feature
        of programmed but thoughtful
subliminal messages of peace, love, and understanding to
        be blown all over the world.

I would like to stockpile all the old noisy leaf blowers, all
        the guns, ammo, missiles,
bombs, and weapons of mass destruction in the world and
        send these instruments of
torture, murder, and mayhem to a place of deconstruction
        without hope of reconstruction
or nuclear fallout or incremental or sudden hearing loss in
        the case of noisy leaf blowers,
that is, the old war blowers.

Blue Speckled Bowl

How shall I house you, blue speckled bowl, too big for my
    cabinets?
And what shall you bear besides cake batter, besides bread
    dough?
I could pick every camellia in Astoria and float the white
  petals in your lake of pink champagne.
I could pile apples higher and higher, and bobbing for Rome
    beauties,
I could drown in you, blue speckled bowl.
Through your looking glass, I see myself grow young, grow
    old, grow young again.

I see JFK, Caroline, and Macaroni.
I see Dorothy, Toto, and the Scarecrow.
I see Ted Sorensen penning words.
I see Dorothy finding Kansas in Oz and Oz in Kansas.
I see Vincent painting cerulean skies.
I see Emily scrawling capitals.
I see the White Rabbit in his checkered coat holding his
    pocketwatch, its glass cracked, its hands stilled.

How shall I house you, blue speckled bowl, too big for my
    cabinets, too big for my yard, too big for the mayor's
    meadow?
You're as wide as the Olympic Peninsula and as deep as
    Crater Lake.
What shall you bear besides cake batter, besides bread
    dough?
Shall I fill you with bricks for all the little pigs?
Shall I fill you with Amish quilts and Hudson Bay
    blankets?

Shall I fill you with stethoscopes?
With corn and turtle beans?
With carrots and artichokes?
With black iron pots for cooking wolves?

Come, answer soon, as the century unfolds;
how shall I house you, blue speckled bowl?

Choose the Card: Four of Swords

Lying on a coffin in a sandalwood cathedral,
you, the knight without armor, dream in daffodiled light.
Your forehead's slick with chrism while
your palms build a steeple above your heart.
Above you, a blue Mary and a red-cloaked child
sing of your three hanging swords,
wanting you to take the fourth one,
rise, and green their blackened ground.

Oh, you want to be that knight
and restore the soil and feed the hungry child,
but considering your likeness sculpted
over a coffin in a perfumed cathedral won't do.
Yes, gentle one, forget the effigy
and that custom which you never understood.
Why celebrate a dead warrior whose rash
valor only cemented corrupt kings and bishops' rule?

But to be another knight, a scribe,
in your own church of words
and witness the other knights
for your brothers' persuasion and warnings true.
First, the slumbering knight, that quivering knight,
who broods and broods
waiting, waiting, waiting for the best possible plan
until surrounding warriors lay him down.
And in contrast, the shadow knight, that cunning knight,
who wisely acts in stealth and outwits the strongest brute.

Choose then, gentle one, your best-knighted self
and will yourself to act
though be your sword a pen
and green your wee ones' blackened ground
and green your wee ones' blackened ground.

One Continuous Line

One night I drew a Buddha head—a
four-inch high, burnt orange ornament
sitting on my desk—though I am not
a Buddhist, I still drew him
in one continuous line from his beaded
headdress to his elongated earlobes to
his rounded chin to his fluid lips curved
neither in a smile nor a frown to his winged
eyebrows across then to his temple and the line
followed line creating shadows, creating halftones,
creating highlights until
it was morning and the pencil drew the side
of my desk, then the wall, and then
the open window where I climbed out with
the paper and I was drawing, still
drawing in one continuous line the redbud
tree, the Japanese maple, my neighbor's hazelnut,
a line of firs and roofs on the slope below out
against the blueberry clouds, the mist rising
up Lookout Mountain, the geese flying above Lake
    Whatcom
and I was still drawing all in one continuous line as my
    fingers
were not my fingers holding a pencil but were one with the
    pencil
continuously sketching more conifers and more flying geese
and an eagle soaring over Lake Whatcom and
the line the continuous line now west of Silver Beach and
up Alabama Hill where a wayward buck slowly
crossed the road until the pencil drew a house and its
    window

and then inside a living room featuring an orchid on a
     table
but then the pencil drew the house's back door, now an open
door, and the pencil drew what was further west in
Bellingham—its flora and its fauna and its rocks and its
     beaches—until
the pencil drew the Salish Sea, pausing a bit on Hornby
     Island
so the pencil could sharpen itself and then head forward
drawing the contours of British Columbia—its
mountains and its valleys and its rivers and its lakes until
days became months became years became decades
until the pencil paused, sensing my coming death—I am
     without sons
and without daughters—until your hand grabbed the
     pencil
as if it were a baton and you with the paper following and
unfurling ever unfurling, yes, you continued drawing
the line the continuous line forming the contours of the
     world.

Acknowledgments

The following poems (some in earlier versions) previously appeared elsewhere, and I thank the editors and readers.

Carretas: "Salmon Have Too Much Press."
ONTHEBUS: "Mockingbird Love" and "The High Priestess Speaks."
inside english: "I Become Go-Go."
Poetry Motel Wallpaper: "With Sweetness and With Ice."
Isis Rising: "The Goddess of Candy" and "Aphrodite Lies Beneath Wisteria Vines."
Carriage House Review: "The Stuffed Bird."
Cirque: "I Live in a Boxcar."
Peace Poems, An Anthology (Volume III): "Go in Peace."

"Blue-White Dress" was featured in the Dress Poetry Show at Allied Arts in Bellingham, Washington, in June 2020. Thank you, Leslie Wharton, for including this poem.

The following poems (some in earlier versions) appeared in my ebook *Snow in Los Angeles* published online in 2012 by Smashwords:

"I Live in a Boxcar," "Let's Make Tea You Said," "The Sea Anemone," "Mockingbird Love," "The Goddess of Candy," "I Become Go-Go," "The Stuffed Bird," "Georgia," "Salmon Have Too Much Press," "My Mother Is a Medusa Monster," "The High Priestess Speaks," "Big-Footed Woman," "Aphrodite Lies Beneath Wisteria Vines," "Your Seventh Rosary," "Red Snowflakes," "Beads," "Shirts," "With Sweetness and With Ice," "Snow in Los Angeles," "Think in Terms of Sunder," and "Blue Speckled Bowl."

I gratefully acknowledge the following individuals for their suggestions regarding many of the poems that appeared in *Snow in Los Angeles* (and now reappear, some in revised form, in this book): Denise Dumars, ellen, the late Mark Henke, and W. Gregory Stewart, all poets from The Shop.

Thank you, Cathleen Long and Tony DiNiro, retired professors from Santa Monica College, for encouraging me in my pursuit of writing poetry.

My sincerest thanks also go to the late Kate Collins and the late Anne Kesslen, both from the English Department at El Camino College in Torrance, California. Their kind words regarding my poetry helped sustain me on my creative journey while I was teaching.

I have attended many poetry workshops, but the following poets and teachers especially inspired me in crafting and performing my poems: Jack Grapes, Gregory SETH Harris, Tere Harrison, Kevin Murphy, and J.L. Wright.

When I moved to Bellingham, several women who hosted open mics welcomed me and encouraged my work. Here's to C.J. Prince from Creekside, Carla Shafer from Chuckanut Sandstone Writers Theater, and Laurel Leigh, a former emcee at Village Books.

I would also like to thank Chloe Hovind and Jessica Moreland of the Fairhaven Village Books publishing team for their assistance with this project.

Finally, I am forever indebted to my husband Lantz Simpson for his unwavering support, for his encouragement, and for his belief in my poetry.

—*V. M.*

Photo Credits

The author gratefully acknowledges the following:

Markus Trienke for his cover photo titled, *Pack Ice in Kulusuk Bay, Greenland, 2017*, obtained through Flickr and licensed by Creative Commons for use with attribution.

Paul McGuire for his photo, *California Palm Tree, Los Angeles, California, 2008,* obtained through Wikimedia Commons and licensed by Creative Commons for use with attribution.

Catherine Wallace for taking the author's portrait.

The author herself shot *Parrotfish on Ice.*

The main text of this book is set in Century.
Italics and **titles** are set in Georgia.

About the Author

Victoria McCallum is a Professor Emeritus at El Camino College in Torrance, California, where she taught reading classes for underprepared students. A Southern California native, she fell in love with the Pacific Northwest at age seventeen while on a family road trip to Vancouver Island. Victoria lived in Oregon for eleven years, earning an M.F.A. in creative writing from the University of Oregon. Currently she enjoys  reading her poetry around Bellingham,Washington, where she has lived with her husband Lantz Simpson since 2016. *Snow in Los Angeles*, her first book of poetry, was e-published by Smashwords. Also a playwright, Victoria co-wrote the book and lyrics for *Catalina Sunshine* with Lantz, and their musical play was performed at the Sylvia Center for the Arts in Bellingham in May 2018. Recently Victoria has written another full-length play called *The Great Refusal*. In this tragicomedy, a talented young painter tries to escape her constricting family, but her disturbed brother pulls her back in.

www.ingramcontent.com/pod-product-compliance
Lightning Source LLC
Chambersburg PA
CBHW060348130626
46553CB00003B/1129